Sunshine

Activity Book 4

W0110742

Erarbeitet von
Inga Bensmann (Weyhe)
Helga Haudeck (Ludwigsburg)
Nadine Kerler (Ulm)
Caroline Schröder (München)

Auf der Grundlage der Ausgabe von
Tanja Beattie
Birgit Hollbrügge
Stefanie Keller
Nadine Kerler
Ulrike Kraaz
Caroline Schröder

scook Deine **interaktiven Gratis-Übungen** findest du hier:

1. Gehe auf scook.de.
2. Gib den unten stehenden Zugangscode in die Box ein.
3. Hab viel Spaß mit deinen Gratis-Übungen.

Dein Zugangscode auf
www.scook.de | 3qbvy-4p7nm

Cornelsen

Contents

Welcome back 3
days of the week, holidays, sports and hobbies

1 A trip to London 5
days of the week, food, sights and transport, the time

2 All year round 11
months and days, numbers, seasons and weather

3 At the museum 17
animals, body parts, directions

4 Keeping fit 23
body and feelings, sports and hobbies

5 Emails from the USA 31
family, jobs, New York, writing emails

6 Looking back at Sunshine 3 and 4 37
words and phrases of all units

Special days 43
Bonfire Night, Christmas, Halloween

Extra: More to explore 47

Word fields 51

Cut-out pages 59

Classroom talk 63

1 Listen. Number the pictures.

2 Where were they in the holidays? Read and draw lines.

☐ ☐ ☐ ☐

holidays in London — holidays in Rome — holidays in Ankara — holidays at home

3 Read the chant. Point to London, Rome and Ankara on the map.

I was in London.
She was in Rome.
He was in Ankara.
And where were you?

4 Talk about the holidays. Ask: *Where were you in the holidays?*

5 Write your own chant. Draw.

I was in ____________

____________ was in ____________

____

____

____

Note
Wochentage werden im Englischen groß geschrieben!

1 Read and number the days in the right order.

2 Two days are on the weekend. Circle the words.

☆ Talk to a partner. Say: *Monday is number …*

☐ Wednesday ☐ Saturday ☐ Tuesday ☐ Thursday

☐ Friday ☐ Monday ☐ Sunday

3 Complete the sentence.

______________ and ______________
are on the weekend.

4 Complete the sentences.

see you · sorry · time

(1) What about playing football on ______________?

Sorry, I haven't got ______ on Monday.

(2) What about watching TV on ______________?

OK. ______________ on ______________

(3) What about meeting friends on ______________?

________ I haven't got time on ______________

A trip to London

1 Listen. Number the pictures.

blue · green · grey · red

2 Read. Complete the sentences. Check with a partner.

Harry is on the ________ bus. The train to London is ____________

Kate's dad has got a ________ car. The underground is __________

3 What is missing? Write or draw.

Make up your own row. Think. Pair. Share.

Note

one bus – two bus**es**

one train – two train**s**

train	bus	car	car	bus	
boat	train	motorbike	boat	train	
taxi	underground	bus	underground	plane	
taxi	plane	train	motorbike	taxi	

1 Listen. Write the missing words.

L 18

bus · boat · car · taxi · underground

1. Kate wants to go to Tower Bridge by  ____________
2. Harry wants to go to London Zoo by  ____________
3. They want to go to Buckingham Palace by  ____________
4. They want to go to Big Ben by  ____________
5. They want to go to the London Eye by  ____________

2 Number the sights.

What day do they want to go to London Zoo, …? Talk to a partner.

3 Where do you want to go? Tick (✓).

4 Ask your partner: *Where do you want to go?* Write.

Think. Pair. Share.

I want to go to …			My partner wants to go to …
	Big Ben	☐	____________
	Buckingham Palace	☐	____________
	the London Eye	☐	____________
	London Zoo	☐	____________
	the River Thames	☐	____________
	Tower Bridge	☐	____________

Look left!

1 Complete the sentences and talk to a partner.

eight · eleven · five · four · nine · one · seven · six · ten · three · twelve · two

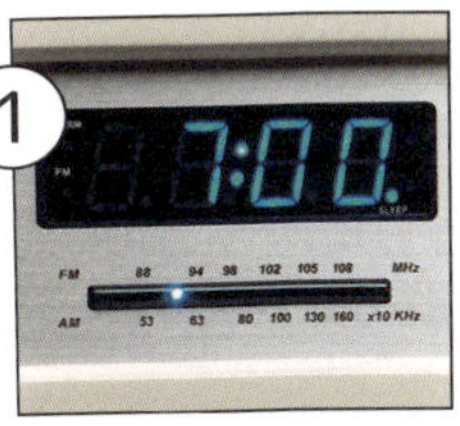

1 ← It is __________ o'clock.

4 It is ______________ →

2 ← It is ______________

5 ______________ →

3 ← ______________

6 ______________ →

2 Plan your day in London. Write down sights and times.

3 Talk about your plan. Where do you want to go at … o'clock? How do you get there?

____

____

____

☆ Make plans for your weekend in London. Pack your bag. Think. Pair. Share.

1 Look at the boat tickets. Read the speech bubbles.

2 Fill in the prices and the times. Check with a partner.

bus	all sights	£2.40	10:45
underground	all sights	£2.40	09:30
boat	London Eye	£	
	Tower Bridge	£	
	Big Ben	£	

Let's go to the London Eye by boat.

How much is it?

It's £3.60.

When is the next boat?

It's at 12:15.

3 Listen. What would they like to eat or drink? L21

4 Read the text. Write the missing words.

☆ Make up your own dialogue.

Harry: A __________ and ____________ sandwich, please.
Man: White or brown ____________?
Harry: Brown, please. And ____________.
Man: Sorry, we don't have chips.
That's £2.60, please.
Harry: Thank you.

bread · cheese · chicken · chips · egg · ham · salad · water

Kate: A __________ sandwich, please.
Man: With or without salad?
Kate: With __________, please. But no _________. And some _________, please.
Man: Here you are. That's £3, please.
Kate: Thank you.
Man: You're welcome. Enjoy your meal!

Portfolio: **Messages from London**

1 Write a postcard.

Look at the note. Write a text message.

Note

How RU? = How are you?
Gr8 = great
KL = cool
Lk = like
Lndn = London
CU = see you

1 Check your English

A trip to London

Ich fand die Aufgabe: ____________________

1 What time is it, please?

____________________ und ich haben uns
(Name)

gegenseitig gefragt, wie spät es ist. ☐

What time is it, please?

It's …

Diese Zeiten haben wir uns diktiert:

________ ________ ________ ________

2 Let us go to Big Ben.

Ich habe mit ____________________
(Name)

das Gespräch mit den Minibildkarten geführt. ☐

Let us go to:

Let us go by:

3 Ich kann diese Wörter für *food / drink* schreiben. ☐

Das möchte ich noch besser können:

____

1 Listen. Number the pictures. (L28)

2 Match the words to the pictures. Write the words.

3 Which two weather words have no picture? Check with your partner.

bike · bus · car · ice cream · jacket · ~~park~~ · shoes · taxi

cloudy · foggy · rainy · snowy · sunny · windy

park ___ ___ ___

___ ___ ___ ___

___ ___ ___ ___

4 Draw the weather. Write.

5 Talk to a partner.

What's the weather like on …?

What's the weather like on the weekend?

I don't know! Let's look at the weather report.

1 Read the temperatures.

2 Write the temperatures. Play Bingo.

3 Explain.

Play again.

Note

three = 3
thirteen = 13
five = 5
fifteen = 15

	Monday	Tuesday	Wednesday	Thursday	Friday	Saturday	Sunday
Game 1							
Game 2							

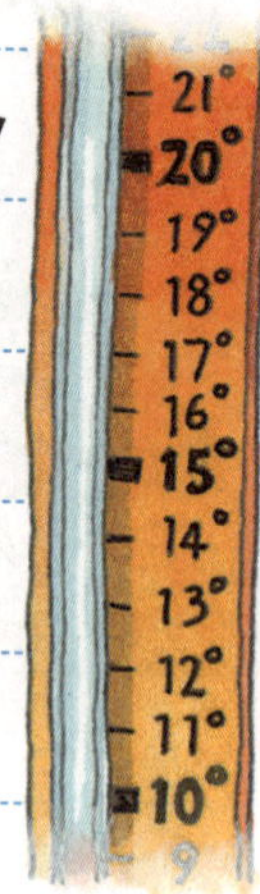

4 Talk to a partner.

What temperature is it on Monday?

5 Read the sentences.

6 Listen and number.

L29

- [ ] Today is Wednesday.
- [ ] Have a nice day.
- [ ] I'm Ted Miller.
- [ ] Here's the weather.
- [ ] Good morning.
- [ ] This is BBC 1.
- [ ] It's sunny today.
- [ ] It's 18°.

7 Write your own weather report. Think. Pair. Share.

This is ____________________

I am ____________________

____

____

____

Note

Make a video.

1 Listen.

2 Read the words.

Find more words. Use a dictionary.

Think. Pair. Share.

Snowdrops in winter
Daffodils in spring
Roses in summer
What will autumn bring?

spring	summer	autumn	winter
 Easter bunny	 swimming	 wind	 snow
 flowers	 sunshine	 pumpkin	 reindeer
 rain	 ice cream	 apples	 pullover

3 Choose words for your chant.

4 Write a chant.

5 Present your chant in class.

Note

Make an audio of your chant.

in spring.

What will bring?

1 Write the months and seasons.

Find more words to match the pictures. Use a dictionary. Talk to a partner.

autumn · spring · summer · winter

January · February · March · April · May · June · July · August · September · October · November · December

Note

December – Dezember
May – Mai
October – Oktober

1 When is your birthday? Write the month and the date.

MON	TUE	WED	THU	FRI	SAT	SUN

2 Complete the sentences.

My name is ______________________________

My birthday is in ______________________ (month)

______________________ (month) is in ______________________ (season)

The weather in ______________________ (month) is ______________________ (weather)

This year my birthday is on ______________________ (day)

3 What is typical for your birthday month? Draw or stick in a picture.

Ich fand die Aufgabe:

1 Chant: Snowdrops in winter

Ich habe ______________ (Name) den *chant*

Snowdrops in winter vorgelesen. ☐ ◯ ◯ ◯

 *in winter.*  *in spring.*  *in summer.*

What will autumn bring?

Ich habe den *chant* auswendig gesagt.

2 What is the weather like on …?

Monday	Tuesday	Wednesday	Thursday	Friday	Saturday	Sunday
______	______	______	______	______	______	______

______________ (Name) und ich haben uns gegenseitig

das Wetter an verschiedenen Wochentagen diktiert. ☐ ◯ ◯ ◯

3 A weather report

______________ (Name) und ich haben uns gegenseitig

einen Wetterbericht vorgetragen. ☐ ◯ ◯ ◯

☐ Monday ☐ Tuesday ☐ Wednesday ☐ Thursday
☐ Friday ☐ Saturday ☐ Sunday
☐ cloudy ☐ sunny ☐ windy ☐ snowy
☐ foggy ☐ rainy ☐ the temperature: ______________

Das möchte ich noch besser können:

____

At the museum

1 Find the words and circle them.

2 Write the words. (Two animals have no picture.)

☆ Draw two more animals. Think. Pair. Share.

Note

Act out the song.
Make a video.

S11 L33 **1** Listen to the song.

2 Number the pictures.

3 What animal is not in the song? Circle the picture.

4 Complete the text.

Sing the song. Do the actions.

~~camel~~ · crocodile · elephant · hippo · lion · monkey · parrot · snake

1. The ____________ is the king of the jungle.
2. The ____________ is big and strong.
3. The ____________ is very dangerous.
4. The ____________ is very long.
5. The ____________ likes to swing through the branches.
6. The camel ____________ likes to walk, walk, walk.
7. The ____________ likes to sit in the mud all day.
8. The ____________ likes to talk, talk, talk, talk, talk, talk, talk, talk, talk, talk, talk.

1 Listen. Complete the sentences. What animals are missing?

crocodiles · dinosaurs · elephants · hippos · lions · monkeys · parrots · snakes · whales

☆ Make up two more dialogues. Work with a partner.

1

Excuse me, please. Where are the ______________?

They're upstairs, in room 31.

2

Excuse me, please. Where are the ______________?

They're downstairs, in room 15.

3

Excuse me, please. Where are the lions?

They're ______________ in room ____

4

______________ ______________ ______________?

They're ______________ in room ____

2 Listen. What animal is it? Fill in the name.

3 Read. Number the sentences in the right order.

☆ Write the rhyme.

- ☐ The ______________ goes
- ☐ He's terribly big
- ☐ And goodness gracious,
- ☐ and he's terribly fat.
- ☐ like this, like that.
- ☐ he has big toes.
- ☐ what a nose!
- ☐ He has no fingers,

____
____
____
____
____
____
____
____

Note

an elephant
a monkey

1 Listen to your partner. Name the animals and the body parts.

2 Write the words.

an elephant's · a crocodile's · a dinosaur's · a lion's · a monkey's · a parrot's

arm · ear · feet · leg · nose · tail · teeth

(1) 

an elephant's leg

(2) 

(3) 

(4) 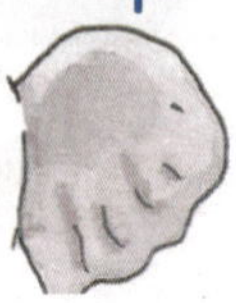

(5) 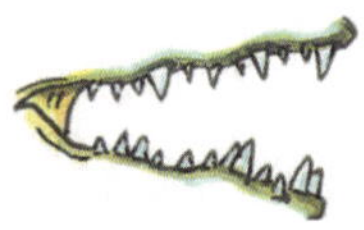

(6) 

(7) 

(8) 

(9) 

3 Where do the animals live? Tick (✓) or cross (✗).

☆ Write more sentences. Draw pictures. Think. Pair. Share.

- ☐ **Monkeys** and **snakes** live in **trees**.
- ☐ **Elephants** and **whales** live in **rivers**.
- ☐ **Parrots** live in the **jungle**.
- ☐ **Crocodiles** live in the **sea**.
- ☐ **Lions** live in the **bush**.
- ☐ **Hippos** live in **rivers**.
- ☐ ______________________
- ☐ ______________________

Portfolio: **Animal presentation**

1 Glue or draw a picture of your animal.

2 Write about your animal.

3 Present.

I want to speak about

___

___

___

___

___

___

___

___

Make notes.

Know your text.

Speak loudly.

Look at the class.

Show pictures.

Check your English

Ich fand die Aufgabe: leicht mittel schwer

☆ Rhyme: The elephant

Ich habe den Reim auf der CD angehört. ☐

Ich habe ______________ (Name) den Reim vorgelesen. ☐

Ich habe den Reim auswendig aufgesagt. ☐

1 Where are the lions?

______________ (Name) und ich haben uns gegenseitig gefragt, wo die Tiere in unseren Museen ausgestellt sind. Wir haben die Tiernamen in die Räume geschrieben (Kopiervorlage 24, Aufgabe 2) und geprüft, ob wir sie richtig eingetragen haben. ☐

2 Talking about animals:

Ich habe ______________ (Name) meine Tier-Portfolioseite präsentiert (Seite 21). ☐

Ich habe mir den Vortrag von ______________ (Name) über ______________ angehört. ☐

Folgende Körperteile des Tieres wurden beschrieben:

arms ☐ ears ☐ feet ☐ legs ☐ nose ☐ teeth ☐

Das möchte ich noch besser können:

____

Note

Viele englische Kinder besuchen einen Schul-Klub. Gibt es so etwas auch an deiner Schule?

1 Read the posters.

2 Work with a partner.
Talk about the clubs. Look at the speech bubbles.

3 Listen. Which club do the children want to go to? Draw lines. (L41)

4 Write sentences.

Emily wants to go to the ______________________________

Kate ______________________________

Samir ______________________________

Harry ______________________________

☆ Which club do you want to go to? Talk to a partner.

1 Read the words.

2 Write the words. Check with a partner.

★ Listen to your partner. Point to the body parts.

arm · back · foot · hand · head · knee · leg · shoulder · toe · tummy

Note

one arm – two arm**s**
but:
one t**oo**th – two t**ee**th
one f**oo**t – two f**ee**t

ear · eye · hair · mouth · nose · teeth

Note
happy ☺
sad ☹

1 Read and number.

2 Listen to your partner. Guess the monster.

☆ Write a text about monster number 4.
Is the monster happy or sad?

1

2

3

4

☐ The monster has got one head, two eyes, one nose, five teeth, four ears, four arms, four hands, four legs and four feet.

☐ The monster has got one head, two round ears, one big eye, two noses, no teeth, two long arms, two hands and two legs.

☐ The monster has got one head, three eyes, one nose, one tooth, no ears, a fat tummy, two arms, two hands and one foot.

3 Draw your own monster. Write about your monster.

☆ Present your monster.

This is my monster:

1 Listen and move. L 44

bend · hop · put · stand · stretch · touch

2 Number the pictures. (Two pictures and words are extra!)

3 Complete the sentences. Check with a partner. Present in class.

arms · hands · head · knee · leg · tummy

1. ______ on one ______

2. ______ that ______

3. ______ your ______

4. ______ your ______ in the air.

5. ______ your ______

4 Make up a new fitness programme. Draw or write.

Act it out.

Note

Make a video of your fitness programme. Use a dictionary.

1 Complete the sentences. Check with a partner.

dance · do judo · play table tennis · ride a horse · ski · swim

Kate can ______________

Emily cannot

____

Samir ______________

Harry ______________

2 What can the children in your class do? Write sentences.

______________ can ______________

______________ can ______________

3 How many children can swim, ...?

4 How do they feel? Write. And how do you feel? Draw and write.

She feels ______________ ______________.

He feels ______________ ______________.

I feel ______________ ______________.

1 Interview your partner. Complete the speech bubbles. (Look at page 27 and 57.)

2 Read the dialogue with your partner. Present the dialogue.

Note

I cannot = I can't

A sports interview

Hi, can I ask you some questions about sport?

Yes, OK.

What's your favourite sport?

My favourite sport is ______________

What about ______________?
Can you play ______________ ______________?

No, I can't ______________.
But I can ______________ ______________

Do you go to the ______________ club on ______________?

No, I go to the ______________ on ______________?

Thanks for the interview. Bye!

You're welcome. Bye!

1 Which sports can you do? Which sports can't you do? Write sentences.

I can ______________________________

____

I cannot ______________________________

____

____

____

____

____

____

____

2 What sports do you love? What sports do you hate?

I love	I hate

What about your family and friends? Write sentences.

____

____

____

Check your English

Ich fand die Aufgabe:

1 Song: Clap, stamp and jump

Ich kann das Lied *Clap, stamp and jump* singen. ☐

2 Fitness in the classroom

Ich habe ein eigenes Fitnessprogramm (Seite 26) erstellt und mit ____________ (Name) noch einmal ausprobiert. ☐

3 Can you …?

____________ (Name) und ich haben uns gegenseitig befragt, welche Sportarten wir können. ☐

____________ (Name) can ____________

4 An interview

____________ (Name) und ich haben ein Interview zu sportlichen Aktivitäten geführt. ☐

☐ dance	☐ do judo	☐ play basketball
☐ play table tennis	☐ ride a horse	☐ run
☐ ski	☐ swim	☐ play football

Das möchte ich noch besser können:

____

Emails from the USA

1 Read the sentences.

2 Listen. Number the answers to the questions (1–5).

L 50

3 Make up two more questions. Find the right answers.

Think. Pair. Share.

- ☐ I'm from Great Britain.
- ☐ I'm 11.
- ☐ It's sunny.
- ☐ In May.
- ☐ I've got 2 rabbits.
- ☐ Thomas.
- ☐ My nickname is Tom.

Note

Dein Name, deine Adresse, deine Telefonnummer oder dein Geburtsdatum gehen nicht jeden etwas an. Sprich immer zuerst mit deiner Lehrerin, deinem Lehrer oder deinen Eltern, bevor du im Internet von dir erzählst. Dein Passwort geht niemanden etwas an!

4 Write the answers.

☆ Make up more questions. Interview your partner.

What's your name?

How old are you?

When's your birthday?

Where are you from?

What's your nickname?

Note

In den USA und in Großbritannien schreibst du die Hausnummer vor den Straßennamen:
50 King Street

1 Talk in class. Ask: *Where are you from? Where do you live? What's your address?*

2 Look at the pictures. Read.

3 Talk about your partner.
Say: *He's/She's from … He/She lives in … His/Her address is …*

4 Write about your partner.

This is Sara. She is from the USA. She lives in New York. Her address is 21 Pearl Street.

This is Sam. He is from Great Britain. He lives in London. His address is 50 King Street.

Note

He's = He is
She's = She is

5 Read the sentences.

6 Write the family words.

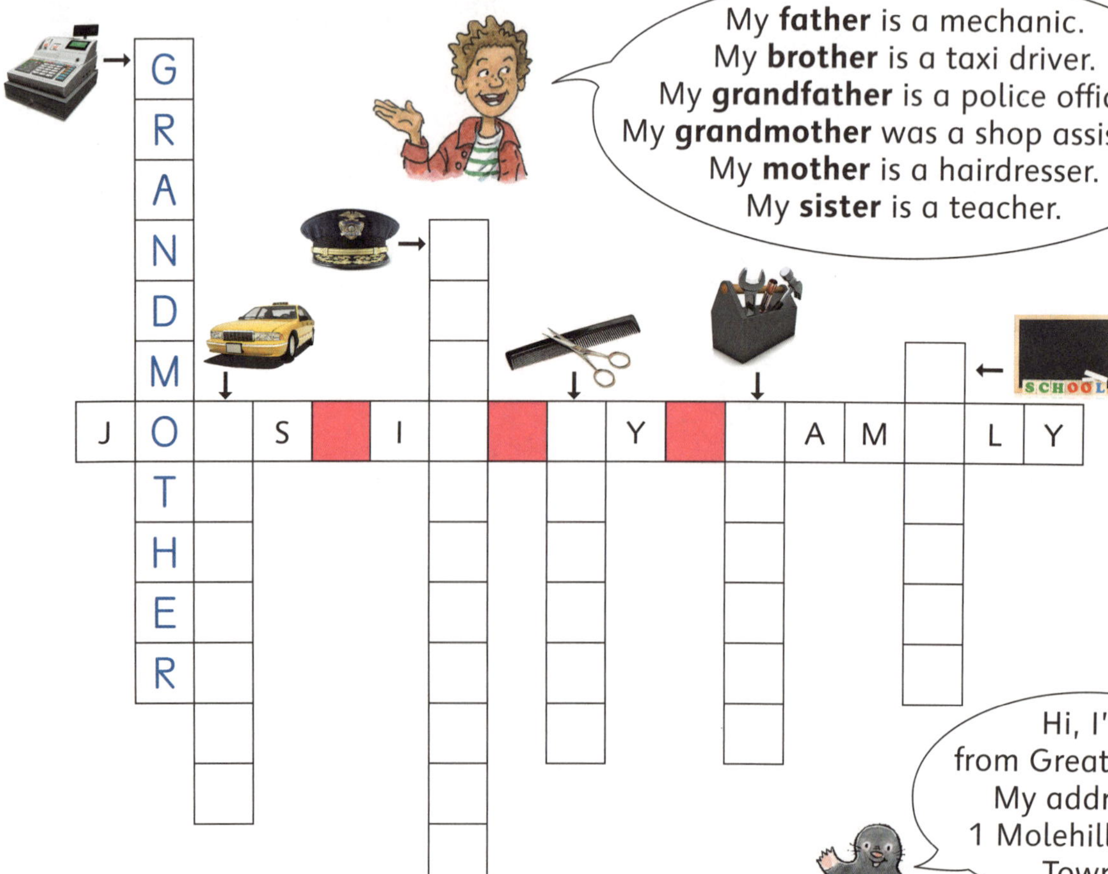

1 Read the words.

2 Write the words.

★ Find more jobs. Use a dictionary. Think. Pair. Share.

hairdresser · mechanic · police officer
shop assistant · taxi driver · teacher

She is a  ____________________

He is a  ____________________

She is a  ____________________

He is a  ____________________

She is a  ____________________

He is a  ____________________

3 Read the words and the text.

4 Write the missing words in the email. Work with a partner.

taxi driver · dog · 11 · Germany · he · May · mother ·
playing with my friends · she · small house

Hi Michael,

I'm from ________________ and I'm ______ years old.

My birthday is in ________. I live with my ____________________ and 2 sisters. My mother's name is Sarah. ______ is a ____________________.

We have got a ____________________ with a garden.

I've got a __________. His name is Rex. ______ is black and white.

My hobbies are ______________________________ and writing emails.

From,

Leon

1 Where does the bus stop? Listen and number.

L 57

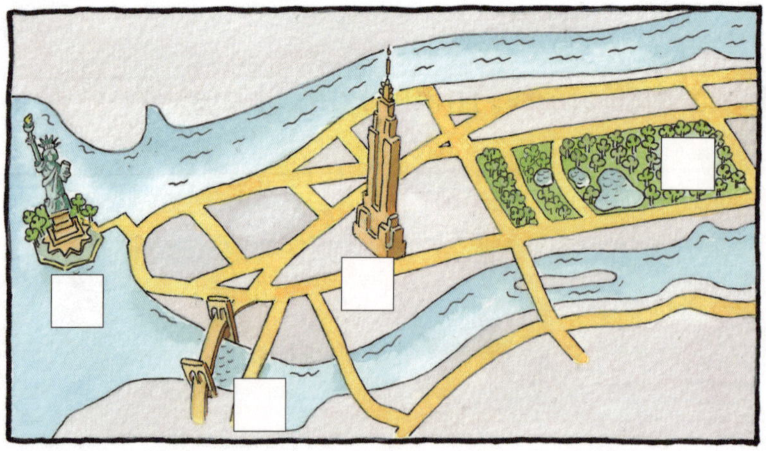

Brooklyn Bridge
Central Park
Empire State Building
Statue of Liberty

2 Write down where the bus stops. Check with a partner.

1. The bus stops at ______________________. Let's have a picnic.
2. The bus stops at the ______________________.
   Wow, what a big building!
3. The bus stops at a river. Over there is the ______________________
   ______________________.
4. The bus stops at ______________________.
   It's a very old bridge.

3 Talk to a partner. Write down the answers.

Name: ______________________

City: ______________________

Street: ______________________

Phone number: ______________________

Mother's name: ______________________

Father's name: ______________________

☆ Who is it? Find out. Work with a partner.

1 Write an email to a friend.

☆ Send your email. Answer your friend's email.

My name is … · I'm … years old. · I've got a … · I'm from … ·
I live in … · My favourite subject in school is … · I'm in class … ·
My teacher is … · My hobbies are … · My favourite sport is … ·
My mum/dad is a … · I like/love/hate … · I don't /love/hate …

New message

To

Subject About me

Hi ______________________________

____

____

____

____

____

____

____

____

____

____

____

____

____

____

Send

Check your English

Ich fand die Aufgabe: leicht mittel schwer

1 Where do you live?

Ich habe gesagt, wo ich wohne. Ich habe

_______________ (Name) nach seiner/ihrer Adresse gefragt. ☐

2 This is Matt's family:

Ich habe Matts Familienmitglieder richtig aufgeschrieben.

Ich habe _______________ (Name) gesagt, welche Berufe Matts Mutter, sein Vater und sein Bruder ausüben.

Ich kann sagen, was meine Eltern beruflich machen. ☐

3 My email

Ich habe _______________ (Name) meine E-Mail auf Seite 35 vorgelesen. _______________ (Name) hat mir seine/ihre E-Mail vorgelesen. ☐

Das möchte ich noch besser können:

____

1 Read the questions. Number and complete the answers.

1. What is your name? 2. How old are you? 3. Where do you live? 4. What is your hobby?	5. What is your telephone number? 6. When is your birthday? 7. What is your favourite subject? 8. Who are your friends?

☐ I live in ____________________

☐ My birthday is in ____________________

☐ I am ____________________

☐ My hobby is ____________________

☐ My friends are ____________________

☐ My name is ____________________

☐ My telephone number is ____________________

☐ My favourite subject is ____________________

2 Look at the board. Write the words.

Is there a pupil in the classroom?

Yes, there is. / No, there isn't.

3 What is in the classroom? Ask your partner. Tick the words. (✓)

☑ pupil ____________________

☐ ____________________

☐ ____________________

☐ ____________________

☐ ____________________

☐ ____________________

☐ ____________________

☐ ____________________

1 Match the words.

crocodile · cat · snake · lion · dog · fish · elephant · hamster · guinea pig · hippo · lion · monkey · rabbit · parrot · whale · rat

 **wild animals** 

 **pets** 

wild animals	pets
______	______
______	______
______	______
______	______
______	______
______	______
______	______
______	______
______	______
______	______

2 Complete the sentences.

dress · jacket · shirt · shoes · skirt · socks · trousers

I like the green trousers, 
the ______________  and
the ______________. 
I don't like the ______________. 

blue · brown · green · pink · purple · yellow

I like the ______________, 
the ______________  and
the ______________. 
I don't like the ______________. 

1 Read the words and sentences.
2 Listen and number the pictures. L 66
3 Write the missing sentences.
4 Read with partners.

Buckingham Palace · Here's the London Eye. · Here's the River Thames. · That was bad. · This is Big Ben. · This is London Zoo. · This is Tower Bridge.

☐ Inspector: What do you know about London?

☐ (1) Pupil: ______________________

☐ (2) Pupil: ______________________

☐ (3) Pupil: ______________________

☐ (4) Pupil: ______________________

☐ (5) Pupil: ______________________

Pupil: And this is … I don't know the word.

(6) Inspector: ______________________

____

5 Read. One word is wrong. Circle.
★ Write headlines. Think. Pair. Share.

clothes · feelings · months · school things · seasons · ~~transport~~ · weather

train	(flower)	boat	bus	transport
dress	pencil	ruler	rubber	______
winter	summer	May	spring	______
windy	sunny	rainy	happy	______
angry	late	happy	scared	______
Tuesday	March	January	June	______
scarf	trousers	oven	gloves	______

1 Look at the pictures. Find the words in the word puzzle (⟶).

2 Write the words next to the pictures.

____

____

____

G	U	I	N	E	A		P	I	G
P	E	N	M	S	T	R	A	I	N
H	A	R	R	Y	H	O	N	E	Y
F	O	O	T	B	A	L	L	I	S
B	I	K	E	T	H	E	R	A	T
S	K	I	I	N	G	T	A	X	I
F	S	W	I	M	M	I	N	G	T
S	U	N	N	Y	A	N	G	R	Y
U	S	S	A	N	D	W	I	C	H

____

____

____

____

____

3 Find more words. Write the words. Check with your partner.

____

____

4 Write sentences.

1

2

3

4

angry · happy · sad · scared

1. The girl is ______________
2. The boy is ______________
3. ______________
4. ______________

Ich kenne englische Wörter aus diesen Themenbereichen:

Das kann ich gut. / Das möchte ich noch besser können.

- family and friends 
- pets and wild animals 
- colours and numbers 1 2 3
- free-time activities 
- school things 
- shopping 
- seasons and weather 
- food and drink 
- clothes 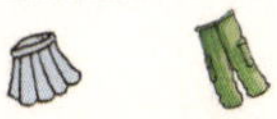
- jobs 
- body parts 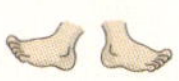

Das kann ich schon auf Englisch:

Das kann ich gut. / Das möchte ich noch besser können.

Sprechen

Ich kann mich, meine Familie und Freunde vorstellen:
My name is … / I'm … years old. / This is my dad.

Ich kann sagen, was ich mag/nicht mag und andere nach ihren Vorlieben fragen:
I like/don't like … / Do you like …?

Ich kann über Freizeitaktivitäten sprechen:
My favourite sport is …

Ich kann im Restaurant etwas bestellen:
I'd like …, please.

Ich kann über meine Lieblingstiere sprechen:
My favourite pet / animal is …

Das kann ich schon auf Englisch:

Das kann ich gut. / Das möchte ich noch besser können.

Hören

Ich kann Fragen über mich, was ich mag und meine Hobbies verstehen:
What's your name? / Do you like ice cream?
What's your favourite hobby?

Kurze Anweisungen kann ich verstehen und befolgen:
Go to ... / Open the book ...
Listen / Point to / Read ...

Ich verstehe den Inhalt von Sätzen, Liedern, Gedichten und Geschichten, wenn Gestik, Mimik oder Bilder mich dabei unterstützen, z. B.:
Harry's night at the museum / Matt's rap

Lesen

Ich kann einzelne Wörter lesen, verstehen und sie Bildern zuordnen, z. B.:
table, pencil, dog, banana, swimming, crocodile

Kurze Sätze,Texte, Lieder oder Gedichte kann ich lesen, verstehen und vorlesen, z. B.:
Elephants are wild animals. / Rudolph, the red-nosed reindeer / Trick or treat / The Earl of Sandwich

Schreiben

Ich kann schon einige Wörter schreiben, z. B.:
cat, blue, sister, tomato, pen, book, jacket, apple

Ich kann einen Dialog vervollständigen:
Hi, my name is ________________.
What's __________ __________?

Ich kann eine kurze E-Mail oder Einladung schreiben:

Dear Harry,
It's my birthday.
Can you come ...?

Hello Kate,
I'm in London ...

Special days: Halloween

1 Number the pictures.

L73 **2** Listen. Write the names.

1: ghost · 2: monster · 3: pumpkin · 4: skeleton · 5: spider · 6: witch

3 Say the words. Draw or write what is missing.

1 Listen to the rhyme.

2 Match the text to the pictures. Draw lines.

3 Say the rhyme. Work with a partner.

Trick or treat,
listen to the beat.

We want only
sweets to eat.

Trick or treat,
smell my feet.

Give me something
good to eat!

4 Make a witch's house for Halloween. You need:

a piece of paper	scissors

1. Take a piece of paper. Fold it in half.
2. Cut off the top corners.
3. Cut out a big door for the witch and a small door for the cat.
4. Cut out a window for the witch.
5. Unfold the paper.

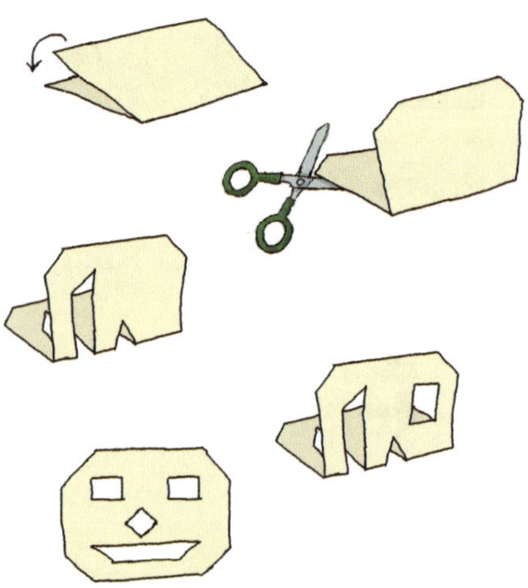

There it is – a Halloween house for the witch and the cat.
It looks just like a pumpkin!

1 Talk about the pictures. Say: *Guy number one is wearing …*

2 Listen. Number the children. (L76)

Draw your own guy. Think. Pair. Share.

3 Draw five bonfires on your London map.
Play with a partner. Where are the bonfires on your partner's map?
Explain the rules.

Is there a bonfire in A2?

Yes, there is.

No, there isn't.

London map A

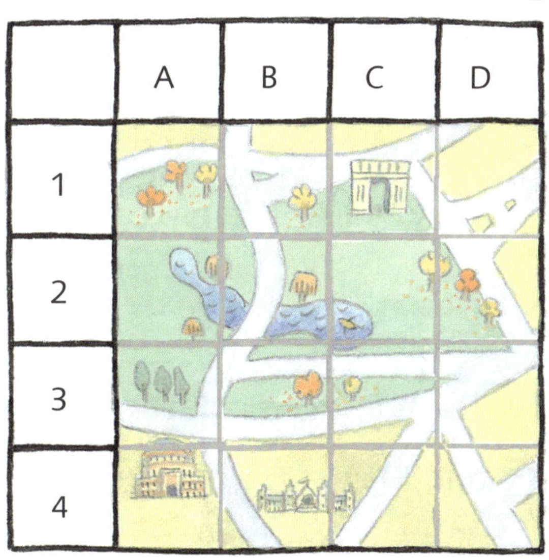

London map B

1 Listen to the song.

2 Read the text.

3 Circle the right word.

4 Complete the text.

Rudolph the red-nosed ________ reindeer · elephant
had a very shiny ________ mouth · nose
and if you ever saw it
you would even say it ________ glows · shines

All of the other reindeer
used to ________ and call him names. cry · laugh
They never let ________ Rudolph happy · poor
________ any reindeer games. play · join in

Then one ________ Christmas Eve foggy · sunny
________ came to say: Father Christmas · Santa
Rudolph with your nose so ________ bright · dark
won't you guide my ________ tonight? sleigh · plane

Then all the reindeer ________ him hated · loved
and they ________ out with glee: whispered · shouted
Rudolph the ________ reindeer, green-nosed · red-nosed
you'll go down in history!

More to explore: The Queen and her family

1 Listen. Point to the pictures.

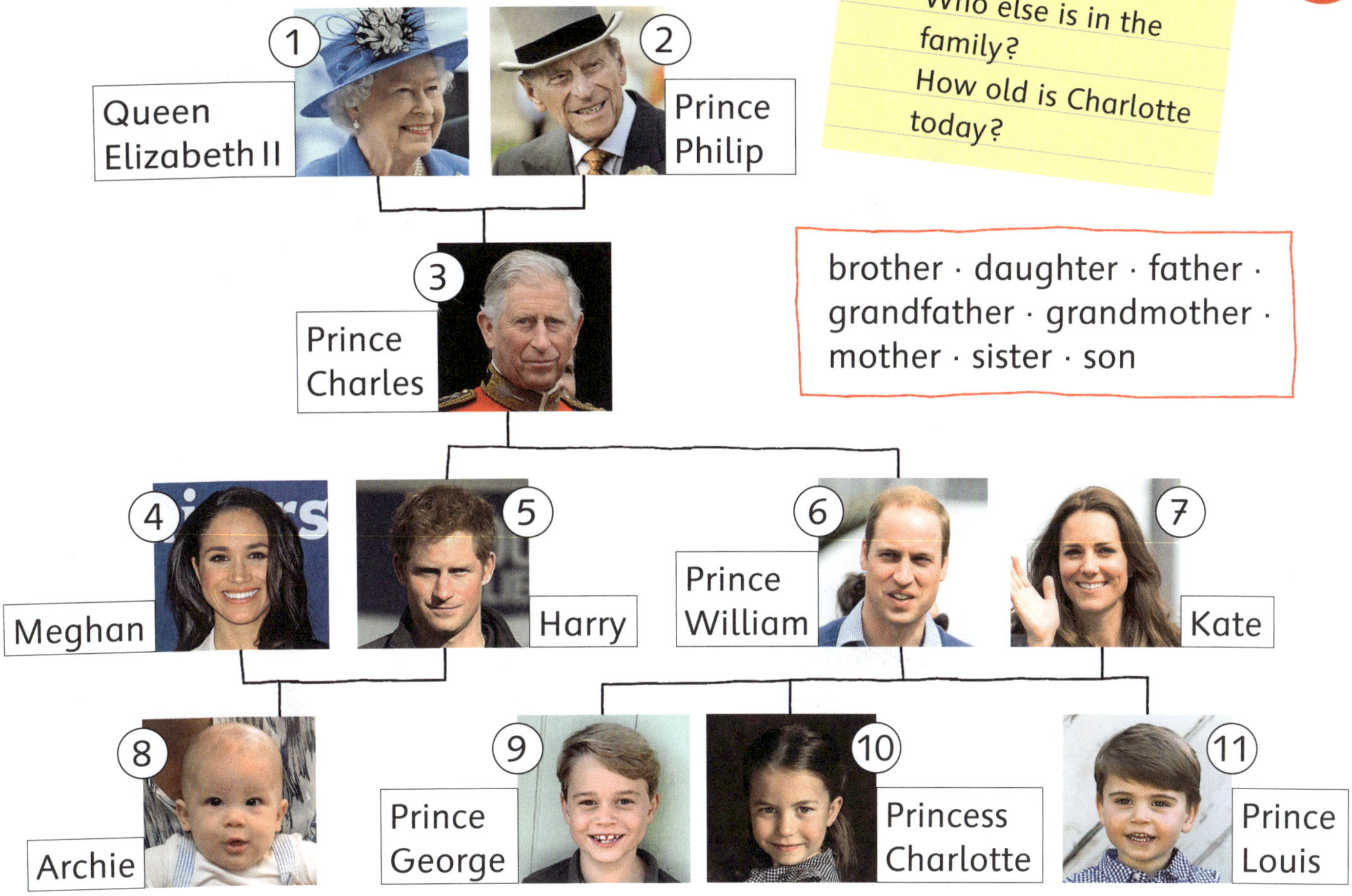

Note

Who else is in the family?
How old is Charlotte today?

brother · daughter · father · grandfather · grandmother · mother · sister · son

2 Number the sentences. Write the words.

3 Write one more sentence.

- [ ] Queen Elizabeth is Prince Harry's ______
- [ ] Prince Harry is Prince William's ______
- [ ] Prince Philip is Prince Harry's ______
- [ ] Kate is Prince George's ______
- [ ] Prince Charles is Prince Harry's ______
- [ ] Princess Charlotte is Kate's and William's ______
- [ ] ______

What about your own family?
You can draw a family tree. Think. Pair. Share.

1 Find the right order. Number the pictures.

2 Tick the right answer. (✓)

	right	wrong
Ben's dad says: 'I'm cold.'		
Ben helps Mr Mole out of the water.		
Mr Mole can fly.		
Mr Mole can't swim.		
The treasure is very small.		

Write one more sentence. Work with a partner.

____

3 Draw the treasure.

Write.

It is a ______________

→ DVD 1

1 Complete the sentences.

Mr Mole: ______________________

What is that?

Mr Digger: It's ____________ bone.

They are at a ____________________

Goodness gracious!

What big ______________________!

It was not ________________ bone.

And it was not ____________ bone.

It was ____________________ bone.

an animal · a crocodile · a dinosaur · an elephant · feet · Goodness gracious! · museum

2 Draw the treasure.

Write.

It is a ______________________

1 Find the right order. Write the sentences. Number the pictures.

fun swimming is

found cross the I

toes your touch

can't we play cricket

2 Draw the treasure.

Write.

It is a ______________________

→ DVD 4

Word fields

Days of the week

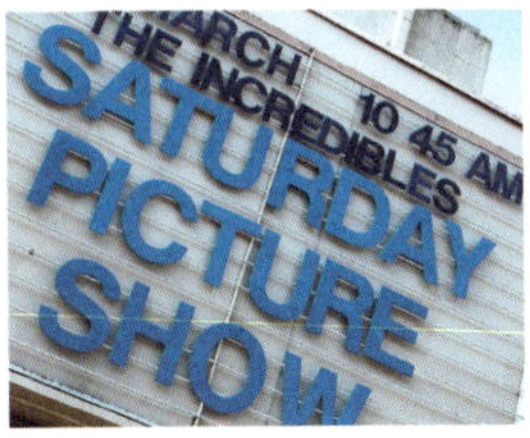

Transport

Days of the week

What about playing football on Monday?

Sorry, I haven't got time on Monday.

Do you have time on Tuesday?

When?

At 3 o'clock.

OK. See you on Tuesday.

My personal words

Transport

When is the next bus to Tower Bridge?

The next bus is at 10:15.

What time is it, please?

It's 3:15.

My personal words

Food

Weather and seasons

Food

I'd like a cheese and ham sandwich, please.

A chicken sandwich for me. With chips, please.

How much is it?

That's £3.10.

My personal words

Weather and seasons

My birthday is in summer.

What's the weather like in summer?

It's sunny and hot.

I was born in winter. It's snowy and cold in winter.

My personal words

Animals

Body parts

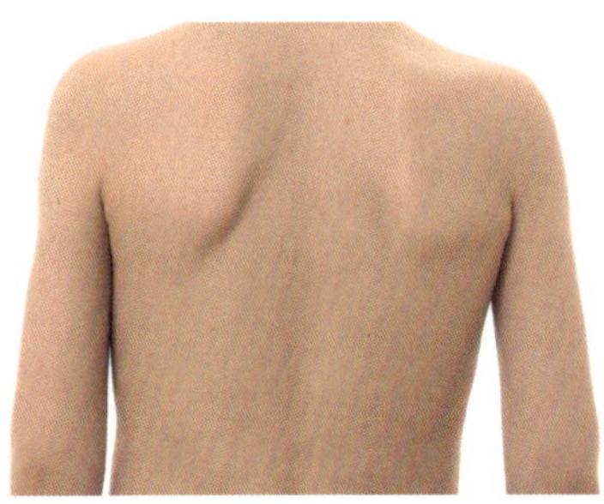
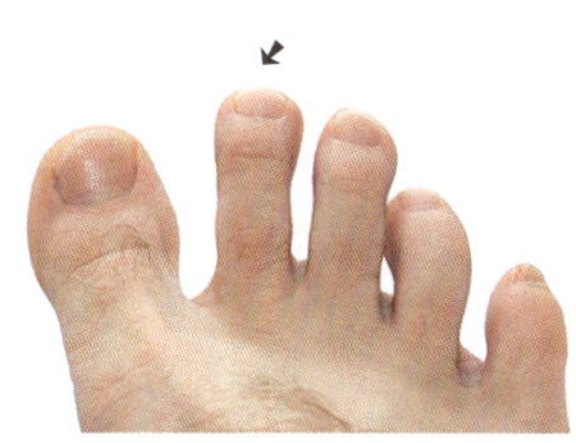

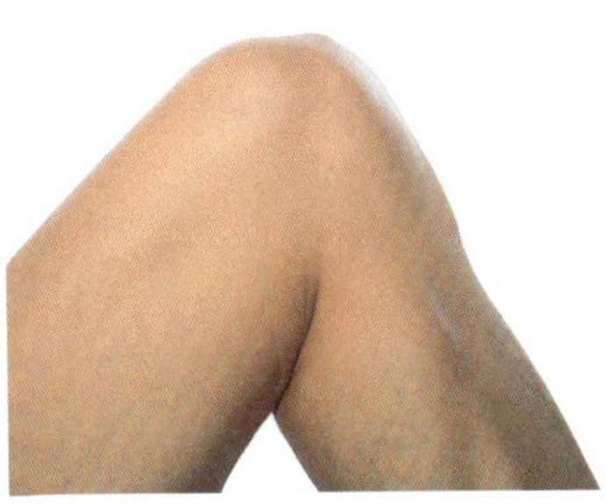
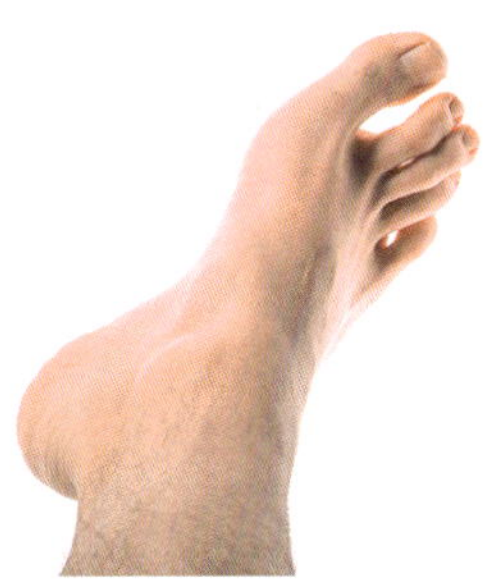
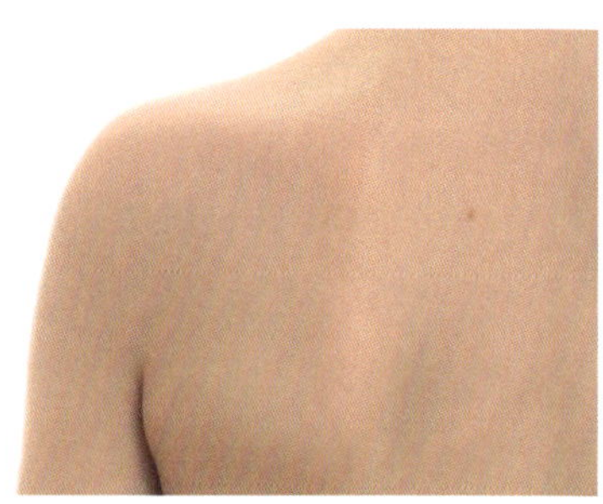

Animals

Excuse me, please. Where are the monkeys?

They are upstairs, in room number ...

What's your favourite animal at the museum?

I like the lions best.

My personal words

Body parts

Stand on one leg, please.

Can you hop to the board?

This is an elephant's leg.

My monster has got a red head.

My personal words

Hobbies and sports

Jobs

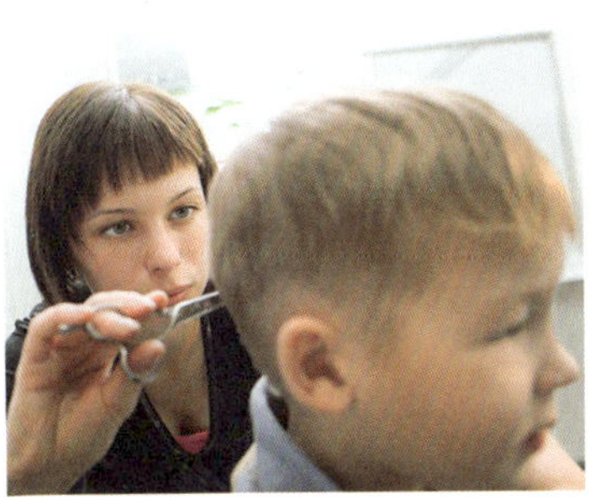

Hobbies and sports

Can you ride a horse?

No, I can't. What about you?

I can ride a horse.

How many children can ride a horse?

My personal words

Jobs

My brother's name is Matt.

What's his job?

He's a police officer.

What's your mum's job?

She's a teacher.

My personal words

What I know in English

1
Guy Fawkes
This book belongs to:
2
London, autumn 1605
Let's kill the king.
3
Yes, let's kill the king with gunpowder.
4
...33... 34...35...36. OK. Let's go.
5
Look at the gunpowder! It's a plot!
6
That's treason!
7
You won't kill the king!
8
Remember, remember
The fifth of November.
Gunpowder, treason and plot.
I see no reason
Why gunpowder treason
Should ever be forgot.

Classroom talk

What my teacher says:

Sit in a circle, please.

Go back to your chair, please.

Open the window, please.

Shut the door, please.

Put your hands up, please.

Clean the blackboard, please.

Let's play a game.

Let's sing a song.

What I say:

Du möchtest zur Toilette gehen. — Can I go to the toilet, please?

Du bist zu spät gekommen. — Sorry, I'm late.

Du hast deine Hausaufgaben vergessen. — Sorry, I forgot my homework.

Du bist mit deiner Aufgabe fertig. — I've finished.

Sunshine

Lehrwerk für den früh beginnenden Englischunterricht

Activity Book 4

Erarbeitet von
Inga Bensmann, Weyhe; Helga Haudeck, Ludwigsburg; Nadine Kerler, Ulm; Caroline Schröder, München

Auf der Grundlage der Ausgabe von
Tanja Beattie, Erkelenz; Birgit Hollbrügge, Bielefeld; Stefanie Keller, Konstanz; Nadine Kerler, Ulm; Ulrike Kraaz, Werther; Caroline Schröder, München

Beratende Mitwirkung
Renate Hafner, Blaustein; Daniela Röbers, Erkelenz; Jutta Rymarczyk, Heidelberg; Siân Williams-Hahn, Schorndorf (englischsprachige Texte)

Redaktion
Daniela Aue-Gehrke, Ariane McIntyre

Illustration
Christian Bartz, Berlin; Beehive Illustration, Cirencester, England (Mike Phillips, Neil Chapman); Raimo Bergt, Wanfried; Volker Fredrich, Hamburg; Mary Hall, Bath, England; Dorothee Wolters, Köln

Gesamtgestaltung
Corinna Babylon

Technische Umsetzung
Corngreen GmbH, Leipzig

www.cornelsen.de

1. Auflage, 1. Druck 2021

Alle Drucke dieser Auflage sind inhaltlich unverändert und können im Unterricht nebeneinander verwendet werden.

Druck: Athesiadruck GmbH

ISBN 978-3-06-084924-6

PEFC zertifiziert
Dieses Produkt stammt aus nachhaltig bewirtschafteten Wäldern und kontrollierten Quellen.
PEFC
PEFC/18-31-166
www.pefc.de

Quellenangaben

Kapitelicons

Kalender: Shutterstock.com/Mega Pixel; Kind: Imago Stock & People GmbH/Westend61; Fußball: stock.adobe.com/Andrey Kiselev; Käse: stock.adobe.com/pinkcoala; Bus: stock.adobe.com/Ludmila Smite; Wecker: stock.adobe.com/Cobalt; Ahorn: stock.adobe.com/Africa Studio; Elefant: Shutterstock.com/pandapaw; Füße: mauritius images/Photoshot Creative; Pfeil: Shutterstock.com/xtock; Familie: picture-alliance/Image Source; Kamm und Schere: stock.adobe.com/odluap; Freiheitsstatue: stock.adobe.com/LittleSteven65; Keyboard: stock.adobe.com/momius; Maulwurf: Lox oder Bergmann; Feuerwerk: Shutterstock.com/Steve Allen; Zweig: Shutterstock.com/n_defender; Kürbisfratze: stock.adobe.com/Pioppo

Bilder

S. 6 (v.o.n.u.): stock.adobe.com/chrisdorney; mauritius images/Loop Images/Adrian Brockwell; Cornelsen/Daniela Aue-Gehrke, Berlin; stock.adobe.com/kmiragaya; stock.adobe.com/Janis Smits; stock.adobe.com/sborisov; S. 7: (Bild 1-6): mauritius images/alamy stock photo/ian nolan; stock.adobe.com/Maksim Shebeko; stock.adobe.com/Bondarau; mauritius images/alamy stock photo/Mike Stone; mauritius images/alamy stock photo/Oleksiy Maksymenko; mauritius images/alamy stock photo/John Bradshaw; Seite: 10 (v.l.n.r.): stock.adobe.com/chrisdorney; mauritius images/Loop Images/Adrian Brockwell; Cornelsen/Daniela Aue-Gehrke, Berlin; stock.adobe.com/william87; mauritius images/alamy stock photo/Justin Kase zfivez; Cornelsen/Daniela Aue-Gehrke, Berlin; stock.adobe.com/kmiragaya; stock.adobe.com/Janis Smits; stock.adobe.com/sborisov; mauritius images/alamy stock photo/Alvey & Towers Picture Library; Shutterstock.com/Michal Rosak; stock.adobe.com/philipus; S. 32: stock.adobe.com/Stefan Rajewski; stock.adobe.com/Evgeny Skidanov; stock.adobe.com/Ad van Brunschot; stock.adobe.com/odluap; stock.adobe.com/Thomas Jansa; stock.adobe.com/DanisNata; S. 35: stock.adobe.com/Maxim Grebeshkov; S. 39 (v.o.n.u.) Cornelsen/Daniela Aue-Gehrke, Berlin; stock.adobe.com/kmiragaya; stock.adobe.com/chrisdorney; stock.adobe.com/Janis Smits; mauritius images/Loop Images/Adrian Brockwell; stock.adobe.com/sborisov; S. 47: (Bild 01-11): dpa Picture-Alliance/PA Wire/empics; dpa Picture-Alliance/REUTERS; Shutterstock.com/Featureflash; Shutterstock.com/Kathy Hutchins; dpa Picture-Alliance/Photoshot; Shutterstock.com/Jean Jeffers; Shutterstock.com/Jean Jeffers; Imago Stock & People GmbH/imago images/PA Images; dpa Picture-Alliance/Photoshot; dpa Picture-Alliance/PA/ASSOCIATED PRESS; dpa Picture-Alliance/Photoshot; S. 48-50: Cornelsen/Puppet Empire; S. 51 (v.l.n.r.): mauritius images/alamy stock photo/Roberto Herrett; mauritius images/alamy stock photo/Jeff Greenberg 0 people images; mauritius images/alamy stock photo/Eric Farrelly; mauritius images/alamy stock photo/Graham Cole; mauritius images/alamy stock photo/Homer W Sykes; mauritius images/alamy stock photo/Jeffrey Blackler; mauritius images/alamy stock photo/Kevin George; stock.adobe.com/philipus; stock.adobe.com/william87; mauritius images/alamy stock photo/Justin Kase zfivez; Cornelsen/Daniela Aue-Gehrke, Berlin; mauritius images/alamy stock photo/Alvey & Towers Pictur Library; Shutterstock.com/Michal Rosak; stock.adobe.com/Dmitriy Sladkov; stock.adobe.com/The Photos; S. 53 (v.l.n.r.): stock.adobe.com/Elena Schweitzer; stock.adobe.com/A_Bruno; stock.adobe.com/otahei; stock.adobe.com/Viktor; stock.adobe.com/Jule-Marigold; stock.adobe.com/PhotoSG; stock.adobe.com/Robert Hoetink; stock.adobe.com/chungking; stock.adobe.com/Gudellaphoto; Shutterstock.com/Ellen McKnight; stock.adobe.com/Bikeworldtravel; stock.adobe.com/Jürgen Fälchle; S. 55: Shutterstock.com/Audrey Snider-Bell; Shutterstock.com/reptiles4all; Shutterstock.com/Maggy Meyer; Shutterstock.com/MartinMaritz; Shutterstock.com/andamanec; Shutterstock.com/aaltair; Shutterstock.com/Michael Potter11; Shutterstock.com/Ethan Daniels; stock.adobe.com/dimedrol68; stock.adobe.com/matka_Wariatka; stock.adobe.com/ schankz; stock.adobe.com/Timo Blaschke; stock.adobe.com//AB Photography; stock.adobe.com/ matka_Wariatka; S. 57: stock.adobe.com/imageegami; stock.adobe.com/st-fotograf; stock.adobe.com/lunaundmo; stock.adobe.com/Pavla Zakova; stock.adobe.com/Artranq; stock.adobe.com/andreyfire; stock.adobe.com/Deyan Georgiev; stock.adobe.com/Firma V; mauritius images/alamy stock photo/Jon Cox; stock.adobe.com/Christian Schwier; stock.adobe.com/Karin & Uwe Annas; stock.adobe.com/danr13; Shutterstock.com/John Roman Images; Shutterstock.com/ ArtWell

Minibildkarten

(v.l.n.r.): Days of the week: mauritius images/alamy stock photo/Roberto Herrett; mauritius images/alamy stock photo/Jeff Greenberg 0 people images; mauritius images/alamy stock photo/Eric Farrelly; mauritius images/alamy stock photo/Graham Cole; mauritius images/alamy stock photo/Homer W Sykes; mauritius images/alamy stock photo/Jeffrey Blackler; mauritius images/alamy stock photo/Kevin George; Transport: stock.adobe.com/philipus; stock.adobe.com/william87; mauritius images/alamy stock photo/Justin Kase zfivez; stock.adobe.com/Dmitriy Sladkov; Cornelsen/Daniela Aue-Gehrke, Berlin; Shutterstock.com/Senohrabek; mauritius images/alamy stock photo/Alvey & Towers Picture Library; Shutterstock.com/Michal Rosak; London sights/Food: stock.adobe.com/Tony Baggett; mauritius images/Loop Images/Adrian Brockwell; stock.adobe.com/giemmephoto; stock.adobe.com/kmiragaya; mauritius images/World History Archive/United Archives; Clip Dealer/Claudio Divizia; stock.adobe.com/stocksolutions; stock.adobe.com/Elena Schweitzer; stock.adobe.com/PhotoSG; Clip Dealer/Givaga; Food/Weather: Shutterstock.com/Nitr; stock.adobe.com/A_Bruno; stock.adobe.com/Jule-Marigold; stock.adobe.com/Gudellaphoto; stock.adobe.com/Bikeworldtravel; stock.adobe.com/Jürgen Fälchle; Shutterstock.com/Ellen McKnight; stock.adobe.com/chungking; stock.adobe.com/Robert Hoetink; Animals: stock.adobe.com/Rhombur; Shutterstock.com/Audrey Snider-Bell; Shutterstock.com/Michael Potter11; Shutterstock.com/MartinMaritz; Shutterstock/Maggy Meyer; Shutterstock.com/andamanec; Shutterstock.com/aalta Shutterstock.com/reptiles4all; Shutterstock.com/Ethan Daniels; Body parts/Sports: Clip Dealer/Sergii Figurny; stock.adobe.com/matka_Wariatka; stock.adobe.com/AB Photography; stock.adobe.com/dimedrol68; stock.adobe.com/Timo Blaschke; stock.adobe.com/tan4ikk; stock.adobe.com/underdogstudios; stock.adobe.com/schankz; stock.adobe.com/matka_Wariatka; stock.adobe.com/Artranq; stock.adobe.com/andreyfire; Sports/Jobs: stock.adobe.com/imageegami; stock.adobe.com/st-fotograf; stock.adobe.com/lunaundmo; stock.adobe.com/Pavla Zakova; stock.adobe.com/Firma V; stock.adobe.com/Deyan Georgiev; Clip Dealer/Discovod; stock.adobe.com/ Karin & Uwe Annas; Shutterstock.com/John Roman Images; Shutterstock.com/ArtWell; mauritius images/alamy stock photo/Jon Cox; stock.adobe.com/Christian Schwier; Halloween/Bonfire: stock.adobe.com/Kzenon; mauritius images/alamy stock photo/Matthew Chattle; stock.adobe.com/Pioppo; Clip Dealer/Andrey Armyagov; Clip Dealer/© www.isselee.de/© www.lifeonwhite.eu; Clip Dealer/Monkey Business Images; stock.adobe.com/iagodina; Shutterstock.com/Cristian Gusa; Shutterstock.com/Steve Allen; stock.adobe.com/Myrna Schwartinsky; mauritius images/alamy stock photo/FLPA

Illustrationen

CHRISTIAN BARTZ U1; U4; S. 10: Teetasse, Wasserglas; S. 25: Notizzettel; S. 41: Geldschein, Wasserglas; S. 44: Papier, Schere; S. 59: Teetasse | RAIMO BERGT S. 3: Landkarte; S. 41: Zahlen, Füße; S. 44: Füße | NEIL CHAPMAN S. 3: vier Urlaubs-Szenen; S. 4: Mädchen; S. 5 (außer Flugzeug, Motorrad); S. 6: Transportmittel, London Eye, Tower Bridge, Zoo, Buckingham Palace; S. 11 (außer Mr Mole); S. 13: alle außer Osterhase, Rentier, Eis; S. 14 (außer Mr Mole); S. 15: Schmuckrahmen; S. 16: Blumen; S. 17: außer Wörterschlange, Schlange und Nilpferd; S. 19; S. 20; S. 21 (außer Junge); S. 23; S. 24 (o.); S. 27 (außer trauriger Junge u.); S. 29: tanzendes Mädchen; S. 32 (außer Mr Mole); S. 33 (außer Verkäufer); S. 34: Stadtplan, Polizeiabzeichen; S. 36; S. 37: Tafel; S. 38: Katze, Meerschweinchen, Hund; S. 40 (o.); S. 41: Katze, Radiergummi, Stift, Wetterabbildungen, Friseurin, Polizist; S. 42 (außer Junge); S. 43 (außer Mr Mole); S. 45 (außer Mr Mole); S. 59: Taxi, Bus, London Eye, Tower Bridge | VOLKER FREDRICH U2: Bastelanleitung; S. 5: Flugzeug, Motorrad; S. 7: blinder Mann und Junge; S. 8: Dialog; S. 9: Hände mit Smartphone; S. 10 (außer Tee, Wasser); S. 12, 16, 30: Mr Mole; S. 17: Wörterschlange, Schlange und Nilpferd; S. 18; S. 21: Junge (o. r.); S. 22; S. 24: Junge (u. r.); S. 25 (außer Notizzettel); S. 26 (außer Mr Mole); S. 27: trauriger Junge (u.); S. 28; S. 31 (o.); S. 33: Verkäufer; S. 34: Dialogszene; S. 37: Klassenzimmerszene; S. 38: Krokodil, Löwe, Elefant, Kinder, Socken; S. 40 (u.); S. 41: Familienbilder, Löwe, Käse, Kinder (u.); S. 42: Junge (o.); S. 44: Junge mit MP3-Player, Mädchen mit Hexenhut, Bastelanleitung; S. 46; S. 48-50: Schatztruhe; S. 59: Mr Mole (mit Tafel, auf Landkarte, mit Union Jack); S. 63 | MARY HALL S. 4, 7, 11, 14, 24, 26, 31, 32, 43, 45: Mr Mole; S. 6: Mr Mole, Taxi; S. 13: Osterhase, Rentier, Eis | MIKE PHILIPPS S. 4: Dialoge; S. 6: Big Ben; S. 29 (außer tanzendes Mädchen); S. 38: Kleidungsstücke (außer Socken); S. 41: Schwimmerin, Fußballer, Rock, Hose; S. 59: Big Ben; S. 61 | DOROTHEE WOLTERS: S. 44: Süßigkeiten

Texte

S. 18 (u.): © Sheila Margaret Ward; S. 46: Johnny Marks © by St. Nicholas Music Inc., USA, Chappell Music Ltd, London W8 5DA Reproduced by permission of Faber Music Ltd, All Rights Reserved, Adm. by Neue Welt Musikverlag GmbH & Co. KG